50 RED FLAGS FOR INTERVIEWERS

DR DHEERAJ MEHROTRA

Made with ♥ on the Notion Press Platform
www.notionpress.com

Contents

Preface

Interviews in today's fast-paced, extremely competitive job market are more than simply a means to an end—they are a two-way street. Candidates should also research the companies and positions they are interested in to ensure they are a good fit, just like employers should do with job applicants. The perfect fit doesn't always materialise in interviews; sometimes, little red flags reveal more significant problems. Candidates can use this book as a practical guide to spot these red flags during interviews and make better professional decisions. This list can help you manage the often overwhelming job-hunting process by pointing out unclear job descriptions, disorganised recruiting processes, poisonous work cultures, a lack of diversity, and unrealistic expectations.

The book **"50 Red Flags For Interviews"** is written to help people feel more prepared and assured when they go into interviews. People looking for work can protect themselves professionally, make decisions that align with their values and goals for the future, and prevent problems if they know to look out for warning signs. Ultimately, a job isn't just a means to an end—it's a promise of personal development, achievement, and meaning in life. If you want to know what's best for your future, this book is for you.

www.authordheerajmehrotra.com

Hiring the right candidate is an art, but spotting red flags is a science. Stay vigilant, ask the right questions, and never ignore the warning signs.

ONE

50 Red Flags For Interviewers

In the highly competitive job-hunting environment, interviews are pivotal for candidates and potential employers. However, not all interviews are equal, and specific warning flags can suggest possible problems inside a firm or within the role itself.

Let us understand the following warning signs that should be observed during interviews to assist candidates in making well-informed judgements on their future career routes.

1. A lack of preparation:

If the interviewer appears unprepared or is unfamiliar with the résumé, this may indicate that the hiring process is not well organised.

2. High rate of employee turnover:

If the interviewer brings up a high turnover rate, this may indicate underlying problems within the management or culture of the organisation.

3. A hazy description of the job

A lack of clarity on the job tasks could indicate that the role is either poorly defined or ever-changing.

4. Comments that are unfavourable or critical of former employees

The interviewer's negative comments about previous colleagues may reflect a poisonous work environment.

5. No provision for the asking of questions

If the interviewer rushes through the interview and does not allow you to ask questions, this could indicate that they are not being transparent.

6. Behaviour that is not professional

An indication of a problematic workplace is when the interviewer makes inappropriate comments or behaves unprofessionally.

7. Avoid Overtime:

When the interviewer focuses excessively on the necessity of overtime, it may indicate that the candidate does not have a healthy work-life balance.

8. It is not diverse enough:

The presence of a homogenous staff may indicate that the firm's culture does not promote inclusivity and diversity.

9. A Reporting Structure:

If the reporting structure is not established, it may result in uncertainty and a lack of direction within the function. No mention of training or development is made at any point.

10. Employee Growth:

If there is a lack of emphasis placed on employee development, it may indicate that the organisation does not invest in advancing its people.

11. Repeated Changes in Leadership:

If the organisation has experienced repeated leadership changes, this may indicate instability and uncertainty.

12. Expectations that are not reasonable:

If the interviewer sets unrealistic expectations for the role, they may cause burnout and unhappiness.

13. Ineffective Communication:

If the communication during the interview process is confusing or inconsistent, it may reflect the firm's broader communication style.

14. A Deficit in the Values of the Company:

The absence of clearly defined values or mission statements may indicate that the company is not moving in the right direction.

15. No Clearly Defined Career Path

If there is no discussion of the possibility of career advancement, this may indicate restricted chances for growth.

16. An Extremely Casual Environment:

A highly casual atmosphere may indicate a lack of professionalism or seriousness.

17. Uncertainty Regarding Performance Metrics:

The interviewer may be unable to clarify how performance will be evaluated, which could frustrate and confuse candidates.

18. Concentrate solely on the salary:

Suppose the conversation is primarily focused on money, without any discussion of perks or the culture of the organisation. In that case, this may be an indication that there is a lack of holistic employee care.

19. The absence of testimonials from staff members:

If current employees do not provide good evaluations or testimonials, they may be dissatisfied with their employers.

20. No Discussion of the Challenges Facing the Company:

If the interviewer chooses not to highlight the difficulties the organisation faces now may indicate a lack of transparency.

21. No provision of References:

This could be a warning sign if the interviewer is unwilling to provide references or contact information for current employees. This could be a red flag if the interviewer refuses to provide references.

22. Rigid Work Hours:

It is possible that the company does not encourage a good work-life balance if the work hours in question are not flexible.

23. Long Hours of Interview Process:

The interview process is very drawn out. If the interview process takes an extremely long time, it may indicate that the hiring team is disorganised or unwilling to decide.

24. Lack of Interaction Within Team:

When potential team members cannot meet, this may indicate a lack of teamwork.

25. Concentrate on Your Personal Life:

Inappropriate personal questions asked by the interviewer may indicate a lack of professionalism on the interviewer's part.

26. The Interviewer Does Not Mention the Company Culture:

If the interviewer does not mention the company culture, it may give the impression that the organisation does not value the topic highly.

27. Uncertainty Regarding the Job Title:

If the job title is ambiguous or deceptive, it may indicate a lack of clarity regarding the role.

28. Restructuring regularly:

It may indicate instability if the company is constantly going through reorganisation events.

29. Inadequate Innovation:

If the organisation does not mention innovative or forward-thinking projects, this may indicate that the company is not moving forward.

30. An Excessive Focus on Loyalty to the Company:

One possible indication of a lack of meritocracy is when the interviewer emphasises loyalty more than skills and qualifications.

31. There is no mention of maintaining a healthy work-life balance:

If there is no discussion of work-life balance, it may give the impression that the organisation does not prioritise the well-being of its employees.

32. Uncertainty Regarding the Expectations of the Job:

Confusion and misalignment may result if the interviewer cannot clearly and concisely define job expectations.

33. A High Level of Pressure to Accept Offer:

If the interviewer pressures you to accept an offer as soon as possible, it could indicate desperation or problems within the team.

34. A Contradictory Discussion of Benefits:

If benefits are not discussed, it may give the impression that the organisation does not prioritise the welfare of its employees.

35. No Opportunities for Feedback:

If the firm does not provide opportunities for employees to provide feedback, this may indicate that the company is not open to making improvements.

36. Uncertainty Regarding the Company's Objectives:

If the organisation does not have well-defined goals or objectives, it may indicate a lack of direction.

37. An Excessive Focus on the History of the Organisation:

If the interviewer places an excessive amount of attention on the history of the organisation rather than its future, this may be an indication of stagnation.

38. Inability to Adapt to Change

If a company does not provide flexible work arrangements, it is possible that it does not support its employees' modern work-life needs.

39. There Is No Discussion of Organisational Achievements:

If there is no discussion of recent accomplishments or successes, this may indicate a lack of growth.

40. An unwillingness to discuss difficulties to be faced:

If the interviewer chooses not to highlight the organisation's problems, this may indicate a lack of transparency.

41. Pay Attention to Our Relationships:

There is a possibility of nepotism if the interviewer places more importance on personal connections than competence.

42. There is no mention of the recognition of workers:

One such indication of a lack of appreciation is the absence of any conversation regarding how employees are recognised or rewarded.

43. Uncertainty Regarding the Location of the Job:

If the employment location is not explicitly specified, there may be uncertainty about whether employees are expected to work remotely or in the office.

44. A Failure to Achieve Social Responsibility:

If the company does not mention subjects such as social responsibility or community involvement, this may indicate that it lacks values.

44. An Excessive Focus on Competition:

The organisation's focus more on competition than collaboration may indicate a toxic work environment.

45. The Tech Phobia:

Suppose the organisation does not mention the technology or tools utilised.

46. The Quality Climate of Organisation:

If now explored of the usage of technology, in that case, this may indicate that the company is still using obsolete procedures.

47. Uncertainty Regarding the Onboarding:

Procedure One potential cause of uncertainty for newly hired employees is a lack of clarity regarding the onboarding procedure.

48. Insufficient Employee Engagement:

If the firm does not prioritise employee engagement, this may indicate that it does not invest enough in its workers.

49. There is no inclusion of the working environment:

The absence of any conversation regarding the working environment may indicate a lack of attention paid to the comfort of the staff members.

50. Having a gut feeling: Believe in your gut impulses:

It is crucial to consider whether or not this is the appropriate opportunity for you if you have any unsettling feelings throughout the interview.

TWO

BONUS

Candidates aware of these warning signs about potential employers can more effectively navigate the interview process and make more educated decisions about their possible joining. Never forget that an interview is a two-way street, and locating a company that shares one's values and professional aspirations is crucial. Long waits without updates are called "no timely feedback."

Role Descriptions That Are Changing: The job description changes after the interview.

Pressure to Decide Immediately: This type of pressure compels you to accept without giving it any thought.

There is a reluctance to provide an official document that pertains to the position.

Conditional Offers: Offers that are contingent on subjective requirements.

Putting excessive emphasis on loyalty once more requires a commitment before beginning.

References are ignored, as the individual does not enquire about or verify references.

Unexpected Withdrawal of Offer: The retraction of an employment proposal for reasons that are not explained.

Uncertain Beginning Date: This prevents the confirmation of a timeline.

Mismatched Offer Letter: The details do not correspond to what was agreed upon in the conversation.

When employees feel a sense of tension or unhappiness, this is an example of a toxic atmosphere.

Gossip among Employees: Employees are vocal about dissatisfaction with the working environment.

Without a code of ethics, there is a lack of transparency regarding company activities.

Pressures to Compromise Values: Encourages dishonesty or taking shortcuts to improve efficiency.

> *"Recognising these warning signs can give you the capacity to make well-informed decisions and guarantee that the next opportunity you pursue aligns with your values, goals, and aspirations."*

About The Author

Dr. Dheeraj Mehrotra, Regional Head of Adani GEMS Education in India, is a distinguished educational leader and innovator with over three decades of experience transforming education through excellence and innovation. A recipient of the President of India's National Teacher Award (2006), he is a certified expert in Six Sigma (White and Yellow Belt), Neuro-Linguistic Programming (NLP), and Total Quality Management (TQM). His specialisation encompasses academic audits, school quality assurance and accreditation (SQAA), and implementing Kaizen and 5S in schools. As an accomplished author, Dr. Mehrotra has published over 200 books on various subjects, including computer science, artificial intelligence, digital body language, quality circles, and school management. His contributions also include the development of more than 150 free educational mobile apps for teachers, students, and parents, a feat recognised by the Limca Book of Records and the India Book of Records. Dr. Mehrotra has served as Principal at prestigious institutions such as De Indian Public School in New Delhi, NPS International School in Guwahati, and Kunwar's Global School in Lucknow. He has also held the position of Education Officer at GEMS in Gurgaon, making significant contributions to the global education community. As a premier UDEMY instructor, Dr. Mehrotra has created over 500 courses that have impacted more than 800,000 learners across 180 countries. Additionally, as the founder and president of the IoT Society of India, he advocates for technology integration in education worldwide.

www.authordheerajmehrotra.com

Books By The Same Author

www.ingramcontent.com/pod-product-compliance
Lightning Source LLC
LaVergne TN
LVHW021259160826
845679LV00001B/130
* 9 7 9 8 8 9 7 2 4 3 0 0 6 *